BROKEN
Rose Petals

Alta Newlun

Broken Rose Petals
Copyright © 2023 by Alta Newlun

ISBN: 978-1639457731 (sc)
ISBN: 978-1639457748 (e)

All rights reserved. No part of this publication may be reproduced, distributed, or transmitted in any form or by any means, including photocopying, recording, or other electronic or mechanical methods, without the prior written permission of the publisher, except in the case brief quotations embodied in critical reviews and other noncommercial uses permitted by copyright law.

The views expressed in this book are solely those of the author and do not necessarily reflect the views of the publisher, and the publisher hereby disclaims any responsibility for them.

Writers' Branding
(877) 608-6550
www.writersbranding.com
media@writersbranding.com

Table of Contents

My Dedications 1

My Blessings 2

My Forever Memories 3

Oh, What A Fool 4

To Be Jealous Is To Be A Fool 5

To My Little Man 6

To Sweet Pea 7

Tears From The Pain 8

Confusion—But Why? 9

The One That Got Away 10

Handsome Guys 11

Tears And Sorrows 12

Baggage Is Meant To Be Burnt 13

The Stranger I Never Know 14

So Misunderstood 15

Drowning In Confusion 16

Growing Pains 17
You Have Only Lies To Say 18
A Box Of Dirty Band-Aids 19
Carry Me Off Lord 20
Allen 21
Great Sadness 22
Allen - 2 23
Arrow Of Truth 24
You're Nothing But A Liar 25
Ears That Can't Hear 26
Allen - 3 27
My Moment To Remember 28
I'm Number Zero 29
You're So Stingy 30
Only To Meet My Father 31
Our Days Are Numbered 32
Your Shiny Soul 33
My Concerning Youth 34
Life Is A Paradise 35
The Absence Of Conversation 36
You Are Settling For The Easy Way 37
To My Sister Of Violence 38
My See Through People 39

My Sister Of Violence - 2 40
Love Is Like A Butterfly 41
Life's Many Lessons 42
Dismissed Like A Melted Candle 43
Your First Love, Her Name Is Alcohol 44
My Sister Of Violence - 3 45
Allen - 4 46
Too Late, I'm Gone 47
Allen - 5 48
So Many Untouchables 49
To My Sister In The Streets 50
My Night And Day 51
My Many Why's 52
All By God's Grace 53
So, I'm An Asshole! 54
So Unkind 55
Broken Princess 56
Very Little Patience 57
You're My Flattered Fool 58
Only God's Sense Of Humor 59
My Only Sunshine 60
My Encouragement 61
You Call Me Sweetheart 62

To My Allen 63
Look Above The Stars 64
Get Hooked On Me, My Name Is Alcohol............65
Hail To Mr. Cannabis..66
Tulio—Why Paint Thinner 67
Crack Kills 68
What's Up? I'm Meth 69
Money Is The Root Of All Evil...............................70
My Unspoken Prayer 71
Why Won't You Change?..72
Allen - 6 73
What Comes Around, Goes Around 74
As Time Passes...75
Allen - 7 76
I'm So Tired Of Waiting..77
Seven Times Seventy 78
Old Past and New Year..79
The Pain of Tomorrow Brings Much Sorrow 80
Why Not You Just Listen? 81
Please Tell Me Why...82
No Pain or Sorrow...83
Busy Birds 84
Precious Silence...85

Feelings Are Like Arrows That Land In The Wrong Direction 86

Only To Be Understood 87

Different, But Same Tears To Me 88

Lost and Trapped 89

A Lost Brother 90

Your Thoughtless Heartbeats 91

The Wounded Bear 92

Lost Time, Always A Regret 93

The Choice I Made And Why 94

No Justice At All 95

The Endless War Of The Poor 96

WHY? 97

Sadness, Always 98

My Darkness To Light 99

Where's The Family? 100

Useless 101

Many Personalities 102

My Locket—Where's The Key? 103

I've Met A Smiling Heart 104

I Call Him Dad 105

You Love Me, You Love Me Not 106

You Ask, But You Don't Receive 107

Lost And In The Past 108

Memories That Don't Matter 109
Don't Waste My Time 110
The Tears Of Depression 111
Your Self Destruction 112
I'm Always Reaching 113
Vodka..114
Easy Money...115
To The Stranger I Just Can't Reach.....................116
Mirror, Mirror, What Do You See? 117
Who am I? You'll Never Know 118
Mr. Almost, But Not Quite Right 119
I Can't Find An Ear To Hear Me 120
The Poison Ones..121
Not A Perfect Life 122
My Eyes See Many Tears.....................................123
December 18, 2010...124
My Season Of Great Pain 125
My Cloud Of Darkness......................................126
Only Not To Be Invisible 127
My Stranger 128
My Twin...129
For My Bear 130
Please Tell Me Why?...131

My Dedications

I feel I've been blessed with many inspiring
and supporting people in my life.
This book I give in honor of my favorite
fan on earth, my grandmother.
My heavenly father who is always with me.

Alta Newlun

My Blessings

My Angel—Lisa Lightfoot
My Sunshine—Mrs. Judy Frey

All of the people of Bessie's House
who believe in me.

For my cover page—Elizabeth Rutschman
Cherith Brooks & Catholic Works

I have been blessed by so many but most
importantly by my heavenly father.

Broken Rose Petals

My Forever Memories

Loving people is never a waste.
Feeling heartbeats is never a loss.
Memories are forever, good or bad.
But, they will always be my memories
to store and keep forever.

Oh, What A Fool

I know tears and I know
disappointments all too well.
Your words are transparent, I see right through you.
So much that I find it funny how you really are.
You never go without, but you seem to forget me.
Someday, will you wonder why
things aren't the same?
Your stupid words "I'll take care of you"
don't mean a thing.
Especially when you forget me.

To Be Jealous Is To Be A Fool

Your jealousy tears me up inside.
I thought you would be different.
It seems when I mention my passion in life,
you tear me up with your words.
Your love for me has limits and I don't
understand why.

Alta Newlun

To My Little Man

You are 22 years old now.
But, I still remember the day I first laid eyes on you.
After waiting for you to arrive a month late,
my beautiful 11lb. 24" blond
hair, blue-eyed baby boy.
I remember you were one of the biggest babies
there in the nursery.
You slept all night when I took you home and
always had a smile on your face.
My little man is now a man and
it seems like yesterday.
I Love You Little Man.

***This poem is in memory of a young lady
who passed in the prime of her life.***

To Sweet Pea

Though I never got to know you, I feel like I do.
I too know great pain and know what it is
not to feel like you exist.
I wish we would have met.
I know we would have had a lot in common.
Your mother understands and loves you,
so you do have lots of meaning and purpose.
You won't be forgotten.
But know you're in heaven with your daddy.
You are a whole person and smiling again
and I know you're by his side talking his ears off.

Dear Sweet Pea, though I never
met you, I feel I have.
July 13, 2011

Tears From The Pain

I feel your pain, I watch your tears fall.
Your life is not what you planned it to be.
Your decisions and changes are so hard to make.
I sit here and think of you.
Old memories come to haunt me so.
I feel your tears and hear your cries.
I wonder why changes are so hard to make.

Confusion—But Why?

Simple lives, unhappy hearts
Simply minds are lost forever
There is no black and white
No two sides of a story.
Now there seems four or five.
Never believe what you hear
and half of what you see.

Alta Newlun

The One That Got Away

You admire the one you lost.
You follow around, honk and flirt.
All that means nothing to me.
I am not a game you can play.
Are you lonely or bored?
I don't care.
I am not your game and I am
not your entertainment.
I'm the one that got away.
I'm your past.

Handsome Guys

To my bear, I miss you so.
Oh, how I wish you had time for me.
You've grown so big and tall.
I miss my guys so much.
I don't understand it all.
It seems our lives aren't going the way I planned it.
Not at all.
I love you guys, I always will.

Tears And Sorrows

In my life there's been many tears and sorrows.
Learn to give it to the Lord for better or worse.
I often wonder about the world today
with many tears for the world tomorrow.
Critical people with ugly hearts and
souls on fire for the world of tomorrow.
Haters will be haters with ugly hearts.
Souls that cry with ugly hearts.

Baggage Is Meant To Be Burnt

Life is how you look at it.
Baggage was made to burn.
Your life is meant to bloom and blossom
like a field of wild flowers.

Alta Newlun

The Stranger I Never Know

They come here for a better life,
but what does that mean?
I'm sure it means different things to me than them.
They come here to a new world,
but they stay in their own world.
I'm sure to them, I'm as strange as they are to me.

So Misunderstood

I don't understand why I can love someone like you.
You turn out to be like all the
other ones I wrote about.
I feel you could never be a part of my world.
They say they're not all the same.
But, I don't.
Why are you so cold?

Drowning In Confusion

It seems that I'm drowning in my own thoughts.
You tell me you'll never give up on me,
But know you say you want to be single.
I ask for things that cost no money,
but you say you don't want to.
I only ask for closeness.
You say you don't want to.
You say you are happy, but I'm not.
I just don't understand.

Growing Pains

I'm not alright, I'm just not fine.
I'm a mess over you two.
I know you're grownups now,
but I miss you so.
When its all said and done, I
am glad I had you guys.
I wouldn't have done it differently.

Alta Newlun

You Have Only Lies To Say

I told you all along, I want forever.
But, I knew forever will never come for us.
When I tell you I'm leaving, you
tell me nothing but lies.
Just to get me to stay longer.
But the longer I stay, the more it hurts.
You tell me what I want to hear,
but its nothing but lies.

A Box Of Dirty Band-Aids

My heart bleeds for you.
You see it pour out, but you have no band-aid
to stop the pain.
I tell you what I want, but nothing
ever seems to change.
When my heart bleeds for you, you only have
dirty band-aids for me.

Alta Newlun

Carry Me Off Lord

Looking back, it seems my whole life
has been nothing but a lie.
From the men in my life that really didn't care.
To the parents I never really had.
But the good Lord has always been there
and always will.
He seemed to always carry me when I just
couldn't walk myself.
And I know He always will.

Allen

Why, when I'm looking for a forever,
I seem to be looking in the wrong direction.
You say you want to be single and
do what you want to do.
Ok, you're free to do just that.
I ask for the simplest thing, but
you're not willing to give.
You seem so selfish and I don't understand.
The only thing that changes is my heart for you.

Alta Newlun

Great Sadness

My heart beats with great sadness for you.
My tears are like rain from the heavens.
It rains with sorrow for you.
Tell me is this what you really want?

Allen - 2

After all this time, you want to be single.
You say you want no boss.
When you said that to me, I gave up thinking
things would change or ever be better.
So, who am I to change that?
I don't even want to try.

Alta Newlun

Arrow Of Truth

You finally shot your arrow of truth
right into my heart.
The arrow said you could never feel the same
about me as I do for you.
You say you want the single life.
Who am I to stop you, I never could !

You're Nothing But A Liar

The ring you gave me is not real.
Just like the feelings you have for me.
Not real at all.
You say you'll change, but in the real world
nobody ever changes. Not even you.
You want what you want.
Well, I won't stop you.
I never really could, could I?
That was all a lie and you're nothing but a liar.

Alta Newlun

Ears That Can't Hear

When I talk, you don't listen.
When I spoke of my feelings,
your ears won't hear me.
All of those "I'm sorry's meant nothing to me.
They were just a lie.
You tell me the truth now and
I promise you I heard you loud and clear.
You don't want the same as I do.
I want forever. You want the single life.
There's really no such thing as forever is there?
It was nothing but lies.

Allen - 3

My broken, tearing heart is all I know right now.
But, this broken heart seems to have so many scars
that it scares her. My heart beats slowly,
because she knows nothing but pain.
The less she beats, the less the pain.

Alta Newlun

My Moment To Remember

To my brother of the streets.
As you stand before me and tell me that you forgave
the man who stabbed you several times
over a loaf of bread.
The Lord told you to forgive him.
That seemed to turn my thoughts and life around.
As you left, I cried out in remembrance of my Lord.
Everything seemed less important.
Thank you brother, that was also for me.

I'm Number Zero

Yesterday was your birthday and oh, what a
day to remember.
It was supposed to be a special
day for us, but it wasn't.
I had a cake and card with a verse I wrote for you.
You were too busy with your
friends to have time for me.
Last night you made me feel like number zero
on your list again. Happy Birthday to you.

You're So Stingy

This morning I finally realized your problems
are not because of me.
Your problems are your own.
Your things you refuse to give to me
that cost nothing to you.
I want your time, your attention.
You are so stingy about that.

Broken Rose Petals

Only To Meet My Father

As the world gets older and so do I,
the summers get hotter, the winter gets colder.
The days get longer, my time gets shorter.
To serve my dear God and to meet my Father.

Alta Newlun

Our Days Are Numbered

The world I live in baffles me.
Many people, many personalities.
Some are strange and some are weak.
Some are young and some are old.
Our days are numbered, so use them well.

Your Shiny Soul

To the flowered lady in my life,
your smile matches the light in your eyes.
Your road has been heard just like mine.
But, your soul shines even at night.
You have been such a shining light to me.

Alta Newlun

My Concerning Youth

The youth of today concerns me so.
You seem to have it all figured out.
That concerns me so.
Your view of the world
is no more than appalling.
Your goals for tomorrow have no value at all.

Life Is A Paradise

The world around me is in chaos.
Drug and alcohol problems all around.
A town full of mental illness.
Every kind you can think of.
Still, life is what you make it.
Life is a paradise.

Alta Newlun

The Absence Of Conversation

I feel better talking to paper,
because you hear only what you want to.
By now, I feel that's how the world is today.
That's all guys ever do.
I try to talk to you about my concerns,
but we never have the same
conversation at the same time.

You Are Settling For The Easy Way

It seems you own my heart,
you tear it in pieces just because
you think you can.
You say you can't do better than
how you're living today.
But I say you're settling for the easy way out.
I'll never settle.

Alta Newlun

To My Sister Of Violence

You're haunted by your past.
Your tears of yesterday seems to
hold back your future.
Stand strong and stand tall.
I know you have a tomorrow.
Dear sister, we have more in common
than you'll ever know
We both keep hoping our guys will change.
But you know that will never happen.
He has to change himself, but he won't.

My See Through People

It seems that in these times
there's what I like to call transparent people.
People you can see right through them.
They act one way around you,
and when they're away from you they be themselves.
I call them see through because
they can only hide from themselves.

My Sister Of Violence - 2

To my sister it's been a long day.
I spent with you and your new black eye.
It was evidence of last night's fight
with your old man of over ten years together.
Over the years I've known you,
I've seen many evidences of "last night's" fight.
And like always it brings back the memories
I try not to remember.
Just remember sis, take one day at a time.
And I love you too.

Love Is Like A Butterfly

How do you let love go?
I think love is like a butterfly.
You let it go to fly away.
If it is truly yours, it flies back to you.

Alta Newlun

Life's Many Lessons

Life lessons are hard to take.
Some are hard and some are long.
Some are easy to learn.
But always remember,
the Good Lord will always be there for you.

Dismissed Like A Melted Candle

Life is like a candle,
it melts away in time.
Just like the hurt you caused me.
It melts my hurt away in time.
It's like the sun shining on a raining day.
I feel last on your list and almost dismissed.

Alta Newlun

Your First Love, Her Name Is Alcohol

I find it hard to compete with your first love.
Her name is alcohol.
It seems when she calls, you come running
with your tail between your legs.
Night or day, and I am left behind
waiting my turn to be noticed.

My Sister Of Violence - 3

Dear Sister,
I talk to you today, we talk about life,
about our disappointments.
Memories we would like to just forget.
As I listen to you, I thought you were
talking about me.
Boy, we have so much in common.

Alta Newlun

Allen - 4

I don't know why,
I feel I lost something I never really had.
All you think about is your next drink
and your next smoke.
I can't get through to you.

Too Late, I'm Gone

Tonight you left me feeling cold
and brokenhearted again.
It seems again and again you will do the same.
Someday you might wake up and say
to yourself I lost the best thing I ever did have.

Alta Newlun

Allen - 5

People tell me I deserve better.
I deserve to be paid attention to
and not forgotten.
Only to be last on your list.
I know this is my life with you.
Why bother.

So Many Untouchables

I wonder how do you reach the unreachables.
Touch the untouchables.
Shed tears for the wounded and the lost.
When there's so much junk to climb through.

Alta Newlun

To My Sister In The Streets

I wonder what keeps you drawn
back to the unknown.
To my sister in the street.
Even thought the streets are no friend of yours,
you keep coming around.
To my sister in the street
That have been wounded and broken down.
And the Good Lord had given you another chance,
but you keep coming around.
I just wonder why? Do you know why?
How many chances will you have?

My Night And Day

I had lunch with you guys today.
I miss you guys so, you are like night and day.
But both just as equal to me.
And after all these years,
you can still bring tears to my eyes.
No matter how old you guys get,
you're still my little boys.
I love you so.

Alta Newlun

My Many Why's

Why do you do the things you do?
Why is your world so much different than mine?
Why do you make me cry?
Why do you hurt me so, you mean the world to me?
All the why's in the world,
wouldn't change a thing.

All By God's Grace

Over the years, life changes us all so much.
We all get older, taller, shorter,
skinnier and even fatter.
But by God's grace, we are all still here.

So, I'm An Asshole!

Today you told me your boss called you an asshole
and you laughed as she left.
You say you were raised by an asshole.
I learned that from you.
It was so you could tear me down.
I earned the right.
I earned the right to be one.
You just want to bring me down.
It won't work anymore.

So Unkind

The world around me seems so unkind.
Every day the crimes of the unkind
walks the streets.
And it seems to lurk around in the darkness
and quiet down in the day.

Broken Princess

Its all about the broken princess.
I don't understand why you need to
get attention that way.
Why can't you discover the talent the Lord gave you?
And why do you keep treating yourself that way?

Very Little Patience

One day at a time is so hard to take sometimes.
I have so much going on right now.
It seems so hard to take.
I have goals and so many dreams.
And I have very little patience,
but my Father understands.

Alta Newlun

You're My Flattered Fool

Today was like so many days of mine.
It seemed like another challenge in my life.
Most people around me seem very difficult.
I come home again with nothing
but despair on my mind.
I open my room.
There on my pillow was a small teddy bear.
For the first time today, I could smile.
I love you my flattered fool.

Only God's Sense Of Humor

People I meet are mysterious, confusing and unique.
No two are the same.
That's why I believe the Good Lord,
had a good sense of humor.

Alta Newlun

My Only Sunshine

My sunshine to you,
all of us are your girls.
You have a hug and a smile for all of us.
Plenty of kind words to for all that need it.
You look at all of us with kind eyes.
You're my sunshine.
I love you so.

My Encouragement

To my fellow artist, you inspire me.
You must have known I needed it.
It's been hard and discouraging for me,
but you have brought great hope
in this old world of mine.
Your music is beautiful, just like your heart.
I hope to return the encouragement to others.

You Call Me Sweetheart

To my partner with the same mission,
you're a hell of a man.
Life hasn't been kind to you,
yet you know what you want.
You talk to me with kindness.
I'll always remember that.
I'm proud to call you my friend.

To My Allen

Someday with the help of the Good Lord,
I'll be important to a lot of people.
It won't matter to me that I was
never really important to you.
I've always been last on your list.
It seems like I am always forgotten.
Why won't you really try?

Alta Newlun

Look Above The Stars

I remember when my boys were young.
They would ask for something they would want.
I would always say, look above the stars baby.
For above the starts lives the answers to it all.

Get Hooked On Me, My Name Is Alcohol

My name is alcohol.
I'll make you spend all your money on me.
I'll make you act like a big jackass.
I make everything so funny.
I make you look stupid to everyone but you.
I'll make sure you won't take care of yourself.
And I will make everyone around you hurt
because of you.
I'll make you forget everything
that's important to you.
Nothing matters when you are hooked on me.

Alta Newlun

Hail To Mr. Cannabis

Hi, my name is Pot.
I'm so cool when I come all grown.
Nothing is wrong with me.
I make you forget all your worries.
I'm so cool, I'll make you not
care about anything at all.
And, I'll have you forget everything
that matters in life.
After I get done with you,
you just won't care.
Remember, I'm Mr. Pot
I'm so cool.

Broken Rose Petals

Tulio—Why Paint Thinner

Oh, Tulio is definitely not a friend of yours.
I watch Tulio turn people into monsters.
He'll make you dumb.
I've known people to get stupid by Mr. Tulio.
He'll even run your life.
I'm Mr. Tulio,
I'm a poor man's out!

Alta Newlun

Crack Kills

My name is crack.
I'm a rich man's drug.
I'll cause you to have a heart attack.
I'll make you too thin.
I'll make you kill for me.
I'll be the death of you.
I'm a rich man's drug.
I'll make you do anything to get me.
You will never see the last of me.

What's Up? I'm Meth

I'm so glad I met you.
Please don't ever figure me out.
I'm mad of nothing but Pure Junk.
I could even unclog your drain.
I'll make you a junkie,
you won't even know.
But remember, I'm your friend.
My name is Meth.

Money Is The Root Of All Evil

Some people, all they think about is money.
And how to obtain it.
Right or wrong it don't matter.
They are doing anything to get it.
Oh, hail to the money.
'Til death do you part.

My Unspoken Prayer

Father, I know you answer unspoken prayers.
You've been with me always.
And I know you'll always will.
I ask you to stand by me.
I'm so scarred and I have lots of
worries on my mind.
And I hurt so.
I want to thank you for sending me
all the people in my life that are truly there for me.
I love them so.

Why Won't You Change?

I cry in silence. You refuse to hear me.
I refuse to show you my tears.
You won't change a thing I know.
I know I can't change you.
You have to want to change yourself.
But, I don't believe you do.
I think you like the way you are.
Don't you want more for your life?

Allen - 6

You seem to have no time for me.
Between work and friends and
your first love, alcohol.
I think its pretty bad that after work
you would rather hang with your friends than me.
It seems that everyone notices me but you.
Why do you want to hurt me so.
I miss the old Allen, the one that used to love me so.
Where are you?

Alta Newlun

What Comes Around, Goes Around

Everything you tell people,
all your lies come back to me.
Only to hit me back in my face.
You break my heart. I tear for you.
Nothing will ever change.
You'll be happy the way you are.
But, I'm not and I don't think you ever loved me.
You just love to lie.

As Time Passes

I always thought as time went by,
we would grow closer.
It seems time is tearing me apart.
I miss you asking me, "How is your day?"
You don't seem to care anymore.
You do nothing but tear up my heart.
Why are you so mean?

Alta Newlun

Allen - 7

Yesterday evening, I came home.
It was the same as always.
I was the last one to get your attention.
I let you know how tired I am of things.
And I meant it.
Again, you probably wasn't listening.
That's alright, my Father does.

I'm So Tired Of Waiting

Why do I always have to wait
for you to have time with me?
I feel we're growing apart.
It seems my forever is never with you.

Alta Newlun

Seven Times Seventy

So they say forgiveness is divine
And that time will heal all wounds.
But you come around me and seem
to carry a crown of thorns with you.
Wherever you may go with the thorns,
you make gashes and open old wounds
that I try so hard to heal.
When I see you around its like
pouring salt in the old wounds you taught me.
And seem to never quite heal all the way.
May someday I learn how to seven times seventy.
And my heart will know it's real.

Broken Rose Petals

Old Past and New Year

To a new day and a new year.
Last year is old and past.
I look forward to the new.
The old is dead and gone.
I look forward to the new.

Alta Newlun

The Pain of Tomorrow Brings Much Sorrow

Oh, what a callous heart you hold.
That causes me so much pain and sorrow.
The pain I bear, I don't deserve.
The Pain you give will be no more.

Why Not You Just Listen?

People can't hear what they refuse to listen to.
The are of conversation is not too clear.
Nobody listens anymore and they sure can't hear.

Alta Newlun

Please Tell Me Why

Why don't we let our kids come home?
Why do we fight the wars of somebody else?
Why do we shed needless blood and pain
for a fight that doesn't end?
Why do we have to lose loved ones
to a fight that needs to end.
Do they care?
Who Cares?
Or, are there just too many of us?

Broken Rose Petals

No Pain or Sorrow

The time of yesterday, tomorrow and forever.
I wish it to bring no pain and sorrow.
The morning tears bring no sun but much rain.
But, rain grows flowers, trees and grass.

Alta Newlun

Busy Birds

Have you ever watched a momma bird
build a nest one twig at a time?
She hunts and builds it
one twig at a time.
Carefully building her babies a home.

Precious Silence

So many words I want to say to you.
But I know they will come out all wrong.
So I chose to say nothing at all.
They say silence is golden.
Sometimes, isn't it?

Alta Newlun

Feelings Are Like Arrows That Land In The Wrong Direction

I don't know why words come out all wrong.
Evil and angry feelings get stirred around.
Sometimes even thrown at the wrong direction.
All I got to say to my past.
Take care and good luck.
I wish you well.
God Bless.

Broken Rose Petals

Only To Be Understood

Many things I like to say to you.
But I know you wouldn't understand.
You didn't understand then and
I know you won't understand now.
So, I choose to say nothing.
Take care and God bless.

Alta Newlun

Different, But Same Tears To Me

You disappoint me so.
But, I am not ready to let you go.
I thought you were different.
But, the only thing different is
the way I think of you, my world around me
and my thoughts about you.
That's what is different now to me.

Lost and Trapped

To my dear with the glass eyes.
I see right through them.
I see your pain.
You feel you're trapped with no where to go.
Pray to the Lord He'll show you where to go.
Have faith and trust He'll show you where to go.

A Lost Brother

To the young man with the crying soul.
You're lost with no where to go.
You get drunk and get high
to mask your pain inside.
You can't see the pain you cause your loved ones.
I'll pray for you just like the other.
I love you and I always will.
Take care and be well.

Broken Rose Petals

Your Thoughtless Heartbeats

You're thoughtless and inconsiderate
to the hearts you wound.
To the hearts you cause to tear,
do you ever wonder why?
You seemed to want what you want
and I am supposed to understand.
But guess what, I don't!

Alta Newlun

The Wounded Bear

To my wounded bear.
Your heart is not whole.
You stay away too long.
I don't understand why.
I remember when you were a small cub.
You were so happy, so loving.
But, now drugs have got you and you've gone away.

Lost Time, Always A Regret

To your past regrets, the choices you made,
they cause you nothing but tears and heartache.
Years go by the choices of regret.
The hearts you've made, the steps you missed.
Your years go by and you wonder why.
Was it worth it you start to ask.
So you ask yourself why.
Why did I miss your first steps,
your first words,
your first missing tooth.
Why? The missing time?

Alta Newlun

The Choice I Made And Why

The wrong choices we make
cause sleepless night and angry days.
Days of tears and sorrow with no hope of tomorrow.
No answers, just questions.
Why did I choose to do this?
And never able to answer why.

No Justice At All

There is no justice for the poor and weary.
I've seen pain and sadness all around me.
People hurt and kill for nothing at all.
People steal and take, just because they can.
Tears of the weary mean nothing at all.

Alta Newlun

The Endless War Of The Poor

The war on homelessness and the poor
mean nothing at all.
The war gets bigger and bigger.
While we get weaker and weaker.
There's no end to this is there?

Broken Rose Petals

WHY?

You are not what I thought you would be.
The arrow of my heart, you missed that mark.
You listen to me, but you just don't hear me.
My hearts hurts for you.
I just don't understand.
And yes, I have tears for you.

Alta Newlun

Sadness, Always

I am saddened by the nothingness
that is wanted by the people of today.
It brings no hope to the people of tomorrow.

Broken Rose Petals

My Darkness To Light

The darkness of night seems so dim.
The light of the sun takes so long to shine.
It's hard to see the shining sun,
when there's darkness all around you.

Alta Newlun

Where's The Family?

When mom and dad aren't parents,
when children aren't kids,
the circle of life gets twisted around.
When grandmas are moms,
and children are adults,
Where's the family lost in this cycle?

Useless

What happened that you just don't care?
What happened so bad that you
just don't care at all?
Do I have no use to you anymore?
Or, did I ever?
Was I always in the way?

Many Personalities

To my lady of many persons.
You have seen so much in your life.
I have great care and concern for you.
Oh, what your life has seen and done.
What you've endured.
What you have overcome.
I don't blame you for becoming many of you.
I think I would too.

My Locket—Where's The Key?

Life's a locket, my heart's the key
Sometimes, life seems to lose the key
that opens my locket.
I have to sometimes through the key away.

Alta Newlun

I've Met A Smiling Heart

To my lady, but dad calls you princess.
Your heart smiles will your eyes allow.
You always seem happy to see everyone.
Even have a hug for most.
When God made you he smiled on your heart.

I Call Him Dad

The man I call dad, I don't even know if he knows,
but his daughter knows.
He's the man that told me he's proud of me.
And even meant it.
Most people call him pastor,
but he means the world to me.
So, I think I will call him dad.

Alta Newlun

You Love Me, You Love Me Not

I love you.
What does that mean to me?
Not a whole hell of a lot.
To you, it means you can do whatever you want
and that's ok.
But, it's not, not to me.
To me, the word love is
used way too much and meant way too little.

Broken Rose Petals

You Ask, But You Don't Receive

Why do you ask me questions,
but refuse to hear my answers?
You ask and expect no reply.
Why do you ask your questions?
You don't want the change.

Lost And In The Past

Do you ever think of me?
Do you ever wonder about your lost one?
Or, do you even care?
Do you remember your little girl that loved you so?
Daddy, do you remember me? I
am the girl that loved you.
Do you remember me?

Memories That Don't Matter

Remember Me?
I'm the one who did all the wrong.
Who couldn't please at all.
I'm the one who always there
and watched when others
could do no wrong, yet hurt you so.
So, I'm the one you tried to cage.
I'm the one you tried to change.
But did you realize I'm just a little
girl who wants you to love her?

Alta Newlun

Don't Waste My Time

Words "I love you" mean nothing at all.
They're just words on paper to fill some space.
They are words on a mirror that can be erased.
Words "I love you" mean nothing at all.
They make you cry, they break your heart.
It make you believe lies.
It means nothing at all.
The words "I love you"
They lie to you and just waste your time.
Why bother, they don't mean a thing.

The Tears Of Depression

I reach for you and you pull away.
I walk to you and you run away.
I cry to you and you laugh
and say there's nothing you will do for me.
There's only tears that fall my way.

Alta Newlun

Your Self Destruction

To my buddy of long ago.
The young man I watched a life time grow.
I know you hurt and I know you
are crying out for help.
But, I just can't seem to reach you.
Once again, you head for destruction.
And all I can do is watch you destroy yourself.
With momma tears, I cry for you.

Broken Rose Petals

I'm Always Reaching

I reach for the sun,
It seems out of reach.
I reach for the moon,
It just keeps me running.
I reach for your love,
But it's hard to find.
I reach for your hands,
but your too hard to hold.
I reach for your heart,
But it's too hard to find.

Vodka

Oh, poor victim,
you're stuck in the past,
you never done wrong.
Oh, poor victim,
you play it well, You hurt everyone,
yet never done any wrong.
Oh, poor victim,
you're never in the wrong.
But, know the only true friend is your vodka.
Oh, poor victim.

Easy Money

Easy money, does that make you happy?
Easy money, does that solve your problems?
Easy money, does that save your soul?
Easy money, makes my heart bleed !
It bleeds for the loss of you my son.
It bleeds for the lost of time with you.
It mourns for the loss of all you can be.
Easy money, shows the weaknesses
in you I didn't know you had.

Easy Money, for who?

To The Stranger I Just Can't Reach

To the stranger, I used to know.
It seems like as time passes,
you just grow old and grey.

To The stranger, I used to know.
Over a century has passed by you and
you're just growing cold as a stone.

To the stranger, I used to know.
I want to know what I did do,
to make you feel this way?

To the stranger, I used to know.
I'm tired and older
and I don't care to try anymore.

To the stranger,
I wish you well.

Mirror, Mirror, What Do You See?

When you look at me and laugh,
who do you see?
A mirror of a person you wish you could be.
Or, do you see another one of your little girls
that don't need you at all?
I'm a life that can go on without you?

Alta Newlun

Who am I? You'll Never Know

Who am I?
In the heart of hurt, the tears you caused.
Who am I?
I'm the one you threw away, when
life does you wrong.
Who am I?
I'm the one that watched all my life.
I'm the one that promised myself,
I wouldn't ever be like you.
I am the one to stop the chain of hurt and pain.
That's who I am.

Mr. Almost, But Not Quite Right

To Mr. almost, but not quite right,
I want to thank you for your strong arms
when I was broken.
I remembered we cried together.
But, I know we're almost, but not quite right.
See, I'm looking for forever.
But, this isn't quite right, because you listen
but you just can't hear me speak to you.
This is not quite right!

Alta Newlun

I Can't Find An Ear To Hear Me

You hurt me when you refuse to hear me.
Or, do you hear me and just don't care?
I used to want forever, but I can't
see you in my today.
What happened to the loving man
who I couldn't wait to see?
He's gone with the seasons,
like summer into winter.

The Poison Ones

People are poison, they're out for themselves.
Not even caring about the hurt and crucified
you caused along the way.
Whatever it takes to get you what you want
is all that matters to you.

Alta Newlun

Not A Perfect Life

To my first born,
I long to make everything in your life perfect.
That nothing in your life will ever harm you,
but know I can't.
I long to see you live happy,
your beautiful blue eyes smile again.
But, I know I can't.
But, I'll pray for you.
I love you my son.

My Eyes See Many Tears

The poorest of the poor,
we're the throwaways.
The forgotten.
What happens to us?
We're the unspeakable,
The useless.

Are we the product of our yesterdays?
We are the hurt,
the torn,
and the waste of today.
And you just push us aside.

Alta Newlun

December 18, 2010

To my little lady, you went home today.
You got to meet our Father in heaven.
I know there will be a day I'll see you again,
but for now, I know you are warm
and you have no more pain.
And, I know you are watching down for us.
And I know you still won't miss a Sunday.
And I know you'll be with us girls on Monday.

Remember, we all miss you and
you'll not be forgotten.

Goodbye, little Martha

My Season Of Great Pain

It seems I'm at war with myself and my mind.
It causes me turmoil and much pain inside.
I pushed my love away.
He tried to hold on, but I wouldn't let him.
Great pain in my mind is too hard to bear.
Even too hard to carry at times.
This load I carry is so awesome.
I do nothing but cry from the pain it causes me.

Alta Newlun

My Cloud Of Darkness

My Season of pain caused great pain and confusion.
At times, its too hard to bear and see through it.
It causes a cloud of darkness with no sun in sight.
My heart beats but, I don't even know why?
My cloud of darkness is a very heavy load to carry.

Only Not To Be Invisible

To grow old and invisible,
is that what life is all about?
Not to be remembered, not to be noticed?
But only to be rejected, old, tattered and dirty?
This world has changed so much today.
We don't have time to stop and look around
to notice the invisible.

Alta Newlun

My Stranger

I just want to thank the very first man in my life,
for all of the changes I need to make within myself.
For never really loving me,
for never letting me be me,
and knowing that's all right who I am.
I thank you for all the hugs I didn't get.
All the praises you forgot to give.
That's all right.
I'll go on.

A. Newlun

My Twin

To my heartless twin, the one that always
made me earn your love and attention.
The one who taught me everything
I didn't need to know
like jealousy, hate, anger and not being enough.
I must thank you for your consistency.
For not giving up.
Your world is not mine, I never want it to be.
I try hard every day to be the person you're not.
Thank God!

Alta Newlun

For My Bear

I seen your girl cry for you today.
On a very special day of the year and you
weren't there for her.
And all she could say is I'm glad I told him
I love you before he left today.
Her tears remind me of mine I had for years for you.
But now they belong to her.
I don't know if I can cry for you anymore.

Please Tell Me Why?

Why don't we let our kids come home?
Why do we fight somebody else's war?
Why do we shed needless blood and pain
for a fight that doesn't end?
Why do we have to lose love ones
to a fight that needs to end?
Do they care?
Who cares?
Or, are there just to many of us?

www.ingramcontent.com/pod-product-compliance
Lightning Source LLC
LaVergne TN
LVHW091555060526
838200LV00036B/850